LOVE~
Your Path to Health

Rudolph E. Grantham

Illustrations by Peggy Cone

Judson Press ® Valley Forge

LOVE—YOUR PATH TO HEALTH
Copyright © 1982
Judson Press, Valley Forge, PA 19481

All rights reserved. No part of this publication may be reproduced, stored in a retrieval system, or transmitted in any form or by any means, electronic, mechanical, photocopying, recording, or otherwise, without the prior permission of the copyright owner, except for brief quotations included in a review of the book.

Unless otherwise indicated, the Scripture quotations in this publication are from the Revised Standard Version of the Bible copyrighted 1946, 1952 © 1971, 1973 by the Division of Christian Education of the National Council of the Churches of Christ in the U.S.A., and used by permission.

Other quotations of the Bible are from *The Holy Bible*, King James Version.

Library of Congress Cataloging in Publication Data
Grantham, Rudolph E.
   Love—your path to health.
   1. Medicine and Christianity—Meditations.
2. Spiritual healing—Meditations, I. Title.
BT732.G7   248.8'6   81-13703
ISBN 0-8170-0938-8   AACR2

The name JUDSON PRESS is registered as a trademark in the U.S. Patent Office. Printed in the U.S.A.

Contents

Introduction   5

THE GREAT PHYSICIAN

  1 Dr. Jesus   9

  2 Jesus Is the Answer to What?   11

  3 The Will to Get Well   14

  4 Meaning and Living   16

  5 Reflections on "Within/Without" and "Spiritual/Physical"   19

THE LOVING TOUCH

  6 Love, Pain, and the Twenty-Third Psalm   25

  7 Loving Someone into Repentance   27

  8 Revising the Chapters of Life Called "Crisis"   29

  9 Cancer Is Not Spelled D-E-A-T-H   31

FAITH HEALING

10 Faith in . . .   35

11 What Do We Expect to Happen?   37

12 The Wisdom Beyond That of Education   39

13 Unbalanced Society and Unbalanced People   42

HEALTHY LIVING AND ILLNESS PREVENTION

14 Jesus, Hygeia, and Aesculapius   47

15 The Illness-Prevention God   49

16 The Message from the Rabbit Town Church Cemetery   51

17 The Good Earth   54

COMPLETING ONE'S HEALING

18 Life Review   59

19 When Tragedy Takes Away a Strength   61

20 When Death Completes a Healing   63

Introduction

When a person is ill, much activity in his or her behalf is performed by others. Those "others" are doctors, paramedical specialists, nurses, and clergy. They are "doing" so much that it seems as if they are in charge. Yet the final responsibility for healing rests with the ill person. Much activity is going on within the person which prevents or slows down or, conversely, permits or speeds up physical healing. At times, when serving as a hospital chaplain, I was acutely aware of patients whose lack of recovery frustrated both doctor and hospital staff. In many of those cases, the patient's physical illness was a symptom of a more pervasive disorder in his or her life. Sometimes a broken marriage had to be healed before the body would allow the person to be discharged to his or her "house" (which was no longer a "home"). The expression of grief or adjustment to an early retirement may have been the prior healing required.

A minister does not "do" a lot of things for people. The healing relationship is one of "being" with persons, helping them understand their lives' meanings, and then supporting them to "do," that is, to live in an appropriate way. The pastor's contribution to healing is very intimate; part of that intimacy is spiritual, involving the patient's relationship with God. People have shared with me their healing experiences. Together we have sought to understand their meaning, in awe when we recognized that the Great Physician had been at the bedside.

This book of meditations has as its theme the belief that love as well as faith and hope are important elements of health. The meditations invite you to shift your focus from the healing work of "others" to your own participation and responsibility. There are personal resources which must be discovered and used. Subjects include the will to get well, exploration of the meaning of one's life and the meaning of one's illness, faith, hope, love, acceptance of oneself and one's situation, commitment, life-style and values, use of timing and of time, and one's personal maturation through life's developmental crises. Also emphasized is the role of church fellowship. Christians bless others through their embodiment of the fruits and gifts of the Spirit. Christian community, one's personal strengths, and the presence of the healing Christ work together, stimulating the body's own healing powers to greater efforts.

This book has several characteristics. Its style is devotional, addressing the mind and the will. It blends traditional faith/intuitive thinking with contemporary rational/scientific thinking. The former thinking process is enough for the pious Christian but is often unacceptable to the secular mind trained in the philosophy of rational humanism.

But medical research in the past few years has affirmed much of the time-honored intuitive/faith thinking on healing. Reading research reports confirming the truths in the "old, old story" has been an exciting phenomenon to me and a valuable tool in my pastoral ministry. Research findings affirm the Bible's message, but they are not ultimate truth superior to revelation. Research that is true is God's truth and will enhance Scripture.

Lastly, these meditations are very personal. People have shared with me their experiences of the presence and work of the healing Christ. With them I have marveled at the encounter, and both privately and with them I have reflected upon the meaning of these experiences. Perhaps this small book is part of the reason these people have shared their intimate spiritual experiences.

I am grateful to the many people who have shared their lives with me. I do not now know the names of most of those whose experiences are included in this book. But to honor any wish that they not be recognized and to preserve their spiritual privacy, I have made slight changes in descriptive details. In some cases permission has been given by the persons to tell their stories for the benefit of others.

THE GREAT PHYSICIAN

1 Dr. Jesus

On one of those days, as he was teaching . . . the power of the Lord was with him to heal (Luke 5:17).

"But if it is by the finger of God that I cast out demons, then the kingdom of God has come upon you" (Luke 11:20).

The woman was in her seventies. Now she was in the hospital with a stroke, pneumonia in both lungs, and a myocardial infarction. She was unable to speak and only awoke occasionally; so near death and with so little life energy left, even resuscitation efforts were believed doomed to failure. We all waited for God to call this saint home.

Only she didn't go "home." Instead, she went to a nursing home! Two days before her discharge she said, "Reverend Grantham, I want to tell you an experience I had. I was lying in bed with my eyes closed. I felt a touch on my forehead. I opened my eyes, but no one was present. I closed my eyes and felt a hand on my forehead. This time I saw a light figure. It was either my sister, who is so close to Jesus, or Jesus himself. I'm not sure. I felt the touch three times."

"How did you feel?" I asked.

"There was a deep sense of peace, and I felt so relaxed that I went to sleep."

I asked if her sister was living. "No, she died ten years ago, but we were very close."[1]

For some people, healing is experienced as a spiritual visitation by Christ. I have been told many stories of his presence and of "turnarounds" in conditions which have been traced to this event. In this case

---

[1] This story is adapted from Rudolph E. Grantham, *Lay Shepherding* (Valley Forge, Pa.: (Judson Press, 1980), pp. 17-18.

the presence of the healing Christ was dramatic, involving the sense of sight and touch. This woman had three illnesses. Christ touched her three times. He revealed himself in a recognizable shape but in a "body" of light. He came in such a way that she associated him with love, both Christ's love and a sister's love. She was left with peace of mind and eventual healing.

Sometimes the presence of God is in a symbol, often a symbol of light. Sometimes he comes in the symbols of a dream. In some cases the dream needs interpreting, but often it is crystal clear.

"How are you today?" I asked a man.

"Fine, after last night," he replied.

"Did something happen last night?" I asked.

"Yes, I had a dream. I awakened and knew that the turnaround had occurred. I've been here for two weeks and was getting worried. But now I know the crisis has passed." The presence of healing powers, whether personified—as in a visitation—or in a symbol or dream, should not be doubted. These experiences bring a conviction that it would be irreverent to question.

Sometimes the revelation is "heard." Once I was tired, overworked, angry, and feeling sorry for myself. I prayed, "God, give me an eight-day week so I can get all this work done." The answer came as a voice saying, "If you can't handle a seven-day week, you surely can't handle an eight-day week."

God's presence often brings peace mingled with joy. When the healing visitation experience is shared with others, it produces in the believer and the hearers a wide range of experiences, such as awe, joy, fear, and a contemplative mood.

"How are you today?" I asked.

The patient responded in a happy, grateful voice, "Thanks to Dr. Jesus and Dr. H. [her physician], I'm getting well."

The next day I saw Dr. H. and told him this. Dr. H., who is a humble, gentle person, replied, "I'm glad she put Dr. Jesus first."

"Dr. Jesus" may be neither highly poetic nor proper for a learned discourse on healing, but it does communicate the reality that an unseen Doctor is at work in our lives. Through personal visitation or through the skills and knowledge of health professionals, we still in our day recognize the truth first announced in Exodus and so perfectly fulfilled in Jesus: ". . . I am the LORD, your healer" (Exodus 15:26).

2 Jesus Is the Answer to What?

Can Jesus, who claimed to make a man "every whit whole" (John 7:23, KJV), do the same for Jane? Jane's[1] life was in a shambles. She was a recent widow at fifty-five years old and a Christian. She felt God, not fate, had dealt her a cruel blow. But her anger toward God was actually a painful symptom of her life adjustment problems and her loneliness. Her circumstances would have been hard enough if grief were all she had to bear.

But there was much more. She was told she was "too old" to be hired. Then there was the auto repair ripoff followed by a new-car salesman's taking advantage of her. As if this were not enough, she was caught up in confusing bureaucratic red tape over her property taxes. Now she was hospitalized because of blackouts, and the doctors were vague as to their cause. At this point she bitterly asked her pastor if *this* was what she had to live for.

To try to comfort Jane with the somewhat glib "Jesus is the answer" would be pouring oil on fire. "Jesus is the answer" may be a comforting generalization to the suffering pious. But this widow demands that one be very specific as to what Jesus has to offer and how one might obtain his benefits.

Jesus anticipated the holistic medical philosophy we see today. Could it be that a study of Jesus' approach to human healing could help Jane?

[1] Jane is a fictitious person used as an example for this meditation.

Just how is the physician Jesus the answer for Jane?

Let us begin with the most dramatic healing of all—resurrection. Jesus restored to physical life a widow's only son (Luke 7:12-15). But focus not upon a demonstration of spiritual power which is almost never seen today, but upon the family's support of a widow.

Jesus' miracle was most likely motivated by his compassion for the widow's circumstances—widows had it even worse in Jesus' times than today. But Jane's son is living. His residence is so far away, however, that he cannot provide the emotional support and the knowledge and skills his mother lost upon her husband's death.

How can Jesus' resurrection of the widow's son be an answer to Jane? The church is a "family." The New Testament calls fellow church members "brothers" and "sisters." A lay shepherding group in her church could "resurrect" this concept (if it is dead) by having church members who are attorneys, mechanics, social workers, etc., serve as consultants to her, volunteering their knowledge. If costly service is desired, it would have to be purchased.

The will to live is related to the will to get well. Jesus asked a man ill for thirty-eight years if he wanted to get well (John 5:6). This would not seem a strange question to those who work in a hospital. It makes a difference for instance, whether a person goes home to a loving spouse or to an empty house. Jane's condition is tied to her feelings of depression and despair over her loss of a partner.

The will to live and the will to get well are related to the meaning of one's life; Jesus must be the ultimate answer in Jane's search for meaning. More specifically, the will to live and the will to get well are tied to the mind and to spiritual factors. Spiritual resources change one's emotions; emotions in turn affect body chemistry. And spiritual resources direct one's activities. A life of service which expresses love and thanksgiving to God for his blessings was praised by Christ (Luke 17:19; Mark 5:19) because it testified to an other-centered life-style. Service to others may even be health-*producing*.

We can say with assurance that this life-style change was one of the *blessings* Jesus gave the insane man living in a cemetery (Mark 5:19). To be given a mission by God is to be blessed. Jane will discover in a life of service an answer to meaninglessness. As she becomes a channel through which God's life flows to others, she will discover a new life for herself. She will want to live and to get well. It is good to love; it is good to be loved.

If Jane's medical tests all come back negative (no tumor, no hypertension, etc.), that is, with no organic reason for her blackouts, then another human healer, the physician of the soul, her pastor, becomes the primary physician. It could be shown that Jane's stressful life situation has brought about a moral "dis-ease" (moral is used in the sense of a break in the faith relationship to God). The moral dimension is not picked up by the physician with diagnostic tests. But Jesus recognized this aspect in healing. He forgave a paralyzed man's sin before he gave the healing command (Luke 5:20). Jane, a Christian, felt she should not accuse God, but she could not help herself. She, therefore, felt guilty and "cut off" from his presence. "Spiritual artificial respiration" might be needed if the moral dimension is to be "cured." And artificial respiration is something done by others. Jane may need a mediator, or at least worship opportunities which offer opportunity for confession.

These different facets in Jesus' ministry of whole healing have touched only briefly on the "how" of "Jesus is the answer." A fuller answer to "how" must be given. But the subject is too involved for adequate treatment here, and only a statement of the point will be given. The best "how" is prayer as practiced by Jesus. He used it as a healing tool.

Prayer for others (intercession) is making ourselves available to God in order for him to do through us what his love and wisdom decide is best. Prayer is not changing God's will. "Thy will be done" is the hardest of prayers. Jane needs the prayers of her friends, and *she* needs to pray. Perhaps a small prayer group would be instrumental in producing the faith healing of God that would touch her whole person: body, emotions, spirit, mind, and meaning with new life. *Jesus is the answer when healing is the need.* And prayer in the Christian community is the "how he is the answer."

3 The Will to Get Well

"Do you want to get well?" is a valid question. Those who work in direct patient care in nursing homes and in hospitals know how important the will is to recovery. "Do you want to get well?" is a question which reaches deep within a person and taps his or her innermost spirit.

The will is intangible and can be easily overlooked. A hospital patient who had been in for several days asked the nurse if there was a chaplain in that hospital. When the chaplain came by the room, the patient said: "I should have called you sooner. But I've been relying on these fantastic healing machines. They cost so much money; it takes so much training to use them, and they cost so much to use . . . why, they have to be good, have to be admired, yes, even worshiped!"

Reinhold Niebuhr's book *Leaves from the Notebook of a Tamed Cynic* comes from the experiences of his early days as a pastor in a Detroit church. After making a hospital call, he wrote in his journal that he felt "like an ancient medicine man dumped into the twentieth century."[1] Niebuhr, like the physicians, focused upon that which can be seen; he missed the unseen factors in his parishioner's illness.

In contrast to the above-mentioned patient was an eighty-one-year-old woman who was in the coronary care unit for a heart ailment and other medical complications. To the chaplain she said: "I'm glad you

[1] Reinhold Niebuhr, *Leaves from the Notebook of a Tamed Cynic* (New York: World Publishing Co., 1969), p. 42.

came by. I'm dying from a broken heart. My son died last year, and I feel God is calling me home through this illness." This lady had centered her grief on her heart and had lost hope for additional life in this world. Her will to live had died. She knew her problem was in the unseen realm of the spirit and sought help from one whose healing specialty was the soul.

O pastors and lay persons everywhere! Would that you had not fallen under the idolatrous spell of healing machines! O children of God, please know that there is no pill or machine or surgery that can heal a broken heart! O members of the clergy, if you only knew how much good you do, you would walk the halls of hospitals as a doctor of the soul and as an equal to those doctors of the flesh. O Mr. Niebuhrs everywhere, awakening the will to live is one of the healing tasks of the "medicine man"!

Jesus asked a man ill for thirty-eight years if he wanted to get well. The man was lying by a pool named Beth-zatha (John 5:2-9). Legend had it that often an angel would stir the waters, and the first person in the pool would be healed. The man stated that he had nobody to put him in the pool. Was the man expecting help from without when he could have found healing from within? The biblical record does not say that Jesus put him in the pool. Indeed, the record does not reveal anything Jesus did for him. He told the man to do it for himself. "Rise, take up your pallet, and walk."

But perhaps there was something of divine intervention in that encounter. At times God heals: ". . . I am the LORD, your healer" (Exodus 15:26). In speaking of Jesus, Luke says, "On one of those days, as he was teaching . . . the power of the Lord was with him to heal" (Luke 5:17). On other occasions Jesus stressed personal responsibility for one's own healing: "According to your faith be it done to you" (Matthew 9:29).

If the former idea of divine healing power "doing for a person" was true, John chose not to emphasize it in the telling of this healing. Instead, we see Jesus stressing the latter idea, the man's personal responsibility for healing: "Rise, take up your pallet, and walk" (John 5:8). Perhaps the truth of a healing encounter is in the principle of cooperation. God's healing power working through the use of the sick person's own will, or through the will of another person, awakens and uses the ill person's dormant healing powers.

However healing works, the question is always valid: "Do you want to be healed?" Healing always begins with the acknowledgment of personal responsibility.

4 Meaning and Living

The woman stood at my door and greeted me. She was a former hospital patient, and I invited her to come in. "I'm alive today because of your visits," she said.

I thanked her for the compliment but knew that her doctor and others on the hospital staff had also worked very hard. I quietly reasoned that I was really receiving her thanks for them as well.

She must have read my thoughts, for she repeated her statement: "I'm alive today because of your visits." This time I realized that she wanted to talk about something very important, and we both sat down. She continued: "I had no reason to continue living. My work was my life. Retirement was a blow to me. My children had their families, and I was not needed and wanted to die. But you helped me find a reason to live."

I've told her story to many persons and have issued a challenge with the telling: "Have you ever considered that knowing the meaning of your life is a healing power? If you are experiencing thoughts like this woman's, I'd like to help you with them. If not I, then perhaps your pastor could help you." Finding the will to live is healing in itself, but the blessing of this reality is equally upon prevention of illness.

Our society's research instruments and procedures seem best prepared for detecting pathology. When a blood sample comes back with normal readings, the doctor orders another test in order to find the pathology!

We hail the successes of medical research and the practical application of laboratory-discovered truths. But other approaches seem necessary if we are to know the life-sustaining potency of such spiritual intangibles as meaning, purpose, and hope. The research instruments and assumptions applied to physical research do not work when investigating spiritual truth.

The research instrument is one's own experience: asking oneself leading questions which are then explored for answers. Dr. Victor Frankl used his own experience in a Nazi concentration camp to explore the questions of meaning and life. Why, he asked, did some people live through unspeakable horror while others quickly died? He concluded that those who lived did so because they had reasons for living. He cites his own research on this very question as a reason for his living to tell his story.

In a less dramatic fashion we all know this experience. A dull job is drudgery, while an exciting one is characterized by energy willingly expended. Morale, energy level, and productivity are the measurements used. Many people verify Dr. Frankl's experience; they, too, live because their work is important to this world and is personally rewarding. Dr. Carl Jung in his autobiography seems to indicate that his recovery from a heart attack was for the purpose of bringing his research to a further stage of refinement.

Experience also tells each of us that it is pleasant to love. We enjoy the experience of giving love, and we enjoy receiving love. The effort expended in loving is not nearly as great as the blessings received. We "leap for joy" and hardly notice fatigue. In contrast, depression is a heavy emotion that "drains" us. A word of condemnation evokes guilt in ourselves and anger toward the condemning person. But being understood by another and receiving forgiveness or patience opens our relationships to mutual enjoyment. There is vitality and zest to life when love, forgiveness, joy, and hope (fruits of the Holy Spirit) are predominant.

While scientific research continues to find answers to its questions, Christians can trust their intuitive faith and the Scriptures that a meaning for living will release life and health in their bodies.

> Now that I am old and my hair is gray,
>   do not abandon me, O God!
> Be with me while I proclaim your power and might
>   to all generations to come.

Your righteousness, God, reaches the skies.
   You have done great things;
   there is no one like you,
You have sent troubles and suffering on me,
   but you will restore my strength;
   you will keep me from the grave.
You will make me greater than ever;
   you will comfort me again.

I will indeed praise you with the harp;
   I will praise your faithfulness, my God.
On my harp I will play hymns to you,
   the Holy One of Israel.
I will shout for joy as I play for you;
   with my whole being I will sing
   because you have saved me.
I will speak of your righteousness all day long.
                    —Psalm 71:18-24*a*, TEV

5 Reflections on "Within/Without" and "Spiritual/Physical"

Possessing the fruits of the Spirit has an effect on our physical as well as our spiritual selves. Love affects us with warm, sometimes exciting feelings; research has discovered that positive body chemistry changes are experienced when one is feeling love. Love is in opposition to fear. Faith seeks belief in trustworthy objects such as God, our physician, and medicines. Hope touches the will and produces a faint feeling of joy, a strong feeling of release and freedom, and a stronger feeling of determination as it calls together and coordinates one's strengths. Hope also incorporates the time dimension, namely, the future. Patience permits us to be satisfied with small gains while we look hopefully to a better tomorrow. The other fruits of the Holy Spirit could also be shown to have healing properties.

Faith, hope, love, patience, and other spiritual gifts are matters first of contemplation and then of action. But our American heritage has bequeathed to us a restless, active spirit. We move our bodies to a new location and opportunity instead of thinking through to new solutions where we now live. This activism is constantly reinforced by law, custom, and habit. Neglected in our American character is the nurturing of those inner processes necessary to healing, to health maintenance, wholeness, and holiness.

There is a normal tension involved here, a polarity of physical/active/outward vs. spiritual/receptive/inner. The time is overdue for correcting the imbalance in this tension of opposites. The tension is seen in such medical questions as: Is the cause of illness "out there" or within the person? Are the cures physical and external to the body (pills, physicians, etc.) or spiritual and within (faith, hope, and love acting on the body's own healing chemistry)?

Medical science illustrates the difficulty of holding these powers in proper balance. In the nineteenth century, two doctors were seeking the reasons people become ill. Louis Pasteur, a French chemist, concluded that illness was due to the invasion of external agents, namely germs and bacteria. Claude Bernard, a physiologist, however, came to a different conclusion. He reasoned that germs are always present but an improper balance in a person's interior environment gives germs a chance to flourish.

Pasteur's germ invasion theory caught on, and today we are well educated to potential dangers "out there" and spend millions of dollars to discover the sources of disease such as cancer-causing agents. Millions more dollars are spent keeping places such as drain pipes and the dark crevices of closets free of outside foes.

Likewise, we diligently look for external agents to take into our body to counteract the external causes of our illness. And since our value structure emphasizes power, we look for stronger headache remedies and more potent therapies that will do the job, but without killing us at the same time. We reason that a physical agent *must* be the healer: pills, surgery, radiation. Our materialistic credo tells us that in such interventions is to be found our healing salvation.

But lately the medical community is examining Bernard's theory that "bugs" don't stand a chance when the body and spirit are strong. And it just may be that the bottom line in this investigation will be that the body itself and one's relationship with others and with God are the greatest source of prevention and healing. For example, the discovery of endorphins, the body's own morphine-like painkillers, lends support to Bernard's theory. Research on stress reveals that one's attitude toward whatever is causing stress is crucial in determining its effects upon the person.

Furthermore, "TLC," that is, tender, loving care, has been discovered to be disease-preventative in rabbits placed under stress, leading us to believe that the same may be true for humans. In an experiment at Ohio State University, rabbits were placed on a high cholesterol diet, and the amount of heart disease caused by arteriosclerosis was measured. One group of rabbits were upsetting the experiment by not getting as sick as the others. Quite by accident it was discovered that a night technician was playing with, fondling, and loving the more healthy rabbits. The experiment was revised. Animals in one group were treated as "impersonal" laboratory animals. Animals in another group were treated as pets. Tender, loving care for the petted rabbits reduced their arteriosclerosis by 50 percent over the other, neglected group of rabbits.

There *are* external agents which contribute to illness. And there are sophisticated chemical therapies, natural herbs, etc., which can be rubbed on, swallowed, and injected. But this is only one part of the "wellness" picture. Harmony of body, mind, and spirit within is also important. And there are also TLC, hope, and faith in God and in others. Somehow these spiritual/emotional energies are received by the body and translated into prevention and/or cure. We have always known that the spirit needed the fruits of the Holy Spirit. Now we have a better idea as to how important they are to the physical body's life.

> Soon afterward he went to a city called Nain, and his disciples and a great crowd went with him. As he drew near to the gate of the city, behold, a man who had died was being carried out, the only son of his mother, and she was a widow; and a large crowd from the city was with her. And when the Lord saw her, he had compassion on her and said to her, "Do not weep." And he came and touched the bier, and the bearers stood still. And he said, "Young man, I say to you, arise." And the dead man sat up, and began to speak. And he gave him to his mother (Luke 7:11-15).

6 Love, Pain, and the Twenty-Third Psalm

Who has not known the childhood experience of being hurt and having a parent kiss the injury so that it did not hurt anymore? Who has not experienced the soothing effects of an arm around the shoulders and the comforting words of a good friend or family member? Did the pain really go away? Or was the experience "merely psychological"? Brain research suggests that pain alleviation is a result of a psychologically induced chemical change.

There is a possibility that the emotion of love increases the body's own painkillers called endorphins. Research in relaxation has discovered that whenever the brain registers a mental image of a part of the body, that part responds to the brain. An anxious dream may aggravate a stomach ulcer. The mind can direct the muscles to relax, and relaxing them quiets the mind's worries and fears!

But what does laboratory research have to do with the devotional life? Doctors have long known that fear produces chemical and hormone changes called the "fight-flight" response. If it is proved that love increases the production of endorphins and thereby reduces pain, can we not also expect chemical changes to be produced by hope, faith, awe, reverence? Can these religious emotions also create body chemistry changes associated with healing? That possibility introduces the subject of prayer.

Autogenics, a form of relaxation often used in pain treatment, utilizes the three components of Christian meditative prayer—relaxation, visualization, and concentration—and adds autosuggestion to them. A product of a research laboratory, autogenics is an interesting blend of traditional religious devotional practice and scientific research.

Let us now move back from present physical reality, which is experienced through the senses, to the timeless spiritual reality recorded in the Bible, experienced today through faith. In *A Shepherd Remembers,* Leslie Weatherhead quotes a letter from a shepherd:

> "'Tis the way of a flock to keep together when they hear the shepherd's voice . . . let some alarm be heard—some disturbance break out, some hurt befall—at once all heads are lifted, all looking, not at the danger, but at the shepherd."[1]

Sheep who stay close to the shepherd's voice and who look at the shepherd when threatened may be teaching us a lesson in faith. Too often we focus upon the problem and become depressed by worry. But meditating upon Psalm 23 or other comforting passages, visualizing in prayer, and studying Scripture—that is, *focusing one's attention on God and his graces*—may prove to be more than "supportive" care. Science may discover what faith has always affirmed: these time-tested and timeless means of grace are healing. Our culture's lack of faith, based on sense verification of reality only, may nullify healing powers in religion as did the negative faith of those in Jesus' hometown where it is honestly recorded: "He did not do many mighty works there, because of their unbelief" (Matthew 13:58).

What is the "bottom line" to all this "coming together" of scientific research and Judeo-Christian religious beliefs and practices? It points to greater use of a person's own faith and responsibility for healing. It points to availability of healing powers in addition to those of surgery and the chemical manipulation of the body. It validates the wisdom of Jesus who regarded pain as an entity to be treated instead of, as in modern medicine, an accompaniment of some other disease or body process (see Matthew 4:24). This should generate a greater interest and participation of the church in healing and illness-prevention ministries.

The next time you are worried, in deep grief, afraid, or in physical pain, engage in a meditation/visualization Bible study using Psalm 23. Use your own favorite translation, or use the highly descriptive translation of Today's English Version.

[1] Leslie Weatherhead, *A Shepherd Remembers* (London: Hodder and Stroughton, 1960), p. 171.

7 Loving Someone into Repentance

The nursing supervisor, seeing me, said, "I've been looking for you; a young man in the end room is crying and wants to see a minister."

The young man was in his early twenties; he had a deep suntan and a good physique. He was a sailor admitted for a foot and leg injury. After brief introductions, he wasted no time telling me his story, beginning with, "Everybody wants to give me a shot, but my leg doesn't hurt. I'm hurting here." He vigorously hit his chest over his heart.

The story of his "heart pain" came tumbling out. He had run away from home as a teenager and had been a wild young man up until the time of his injury. He loved and cared for no one. What is more, he felt he deserved no one's love. But in two days in the hospital, he had been showered with love from his parents, hospital employees, a hospital volunteer, and his ship's crew.

The biggest shock came when a huge, rough, tattooed crewman visited him. He had been told to keep away from this "mean man." He had. Now this rough-looking sailor had come to visit. He told about his own young, wild life, how his hard drinking and brawling shore leaves had created problems for him. He concluded his story by telling how Jesus had changed his life. "Jesus can change your life too," he said. Furthermore, he reminded the young sailor how close he had come to death. The young sailor concluded his story with, "I don't deserve all this love!'' and wanted to know how people could be this way toward him.

From that opening we discussed the forgiving love of Christ and how Christians are compelled to love as Christ loves them. We then talked about prayer as a means of spiritual relationship. I gave him two brochures on prayer and a New Testament. There were other visits; I hope he has continued in his new spiritual life.

There are several lessons to be drawn from this story. Many people think conversion has to be effected by "hell fire" warnings. This young man would never have responded to guilt-raising evangelism. But he could not resist unmerited love that asked nothing in return.

When a person is in a hospital, we usually think of healing in physical terms and stop there. But healing is more than body repair work. This young man could have gotten well and returned to a wild life dangerous to himself and others, as well as unproductive to society in general. Whole healing must affect one's motivations, values, and life-style. This young sailor's experience reflects this holistic understanding of healing.

Most American hospital care is provided in a secular context. And many of the nursing and healing skills that are practiced stand independent of the practitioner's moral or spiritual code. But Christians seek and find opportunities to live their faith. In the case of this young man, a nursing supervisor, a nurse, a volunteer, and a unit clerk saw this man's spiritual need and asked me, the chaplain, to see a young man with an injured leg but whose pain was in the heart. Healing "took" in both places because people who have been loved by Christ love as he loves.

> "A new commandment I give to you, that you love one another; even as I have loved you, that you also love one another. By this all men will know that you are my disciples, if you have love for one another" (John 13:34-35).

8 Revising the Chapters of Life Called "Crisis"

> *But you are a chosen race, a royal priesthood, a holy nation, God's own people, that you may declare the wonderful deeds of him who called you out of darkness into his marvelous light. Once you were no people but now you are God's people; once you had not received mercy but now you have received mercy. . . . Finally, all of you, have unity of spirit, sympathy, love of the brethren, a tender heart and a humble mind* (1 Peter 2:9-10; 3:8).

One's life is like a book. And, like a book, it has many chapters. Some are comedies; some tragedies; some mixed. Chapters might be called "Childhood," "The Turbulent Teens," "Two Becoming One," "The Empty Nest," or "Going It Alone." It is hoped that redemptive love, expressed through the church, God's royal priesthood, is present in all.

Sometimes a chapter is brought to a close by the physical, emotional, social, or spiritual developmental process. It routinely closes, perhaps with a bit of anxiety (grief or birth trauma?), but otherwise the transition is smooth and hardly noticed. Later we may look back with nostalgia, which is probably residual grief. But for many of us life moves ahead smoothly.

Occasionally, though, a chapter is brought to a close by a traumatic event: an accident snuffs out a mate's life or a stroke or heart attack forces one into an early retirement. The trauma is severe, the anguish deep. The "why, God?" becomes insistent, angry in tone, or desperately pleading. Life's routine and meaning are torn, and we must find ourselves again. The next chapter in this personal autobiography is costly in terms of personal life adjustment and emotional pain. These chapters could be called "Adjusting to a Heart Attack," "Mastering a New Vocation," "Too Young to Sit on My Hands," or "Slow Deterioration Till Death." The pain seems permanent, the grief unrelieved; hope crushed to earth seems never to rise again. It is in these crisis chapters that the benefits of routine Sunday school and church attendance and "sunny day" prayers are put to the test. The storm is howling; will the roots hold? The limbs are being stripped away; will the tree itself survive?

Crises which become chronic are the church's opportunity to show its colors. The church as a support community has always been in the business of crisis intervention—its founder was present with the poor, outcast, and sick. But when the crisis moves into a chronic life-style of need and deprivation, the church, Christ's body, continues to sustain and, beyond that, leads to new and better life.

There are many helpers, professional and lay, who stand between the chapters of life. They say to all who will hear: "I'm available, and my philosophy and therapy and machines are effective." We thank God for all helpers whether they are working in a "secular" or "sacred" context. Indeed, in many cases these helpers are the church in the world; for if it is love, it is of God. If it is healing, it is from the Great Physician. But the church has a unique role many crisis helpers do not. It was present before the crisis in prior chapters of life. It assists the transition between chapters and will help write the following ones. The church knows its people's strengths and can enforce and mobilize them. It will also assist at the person's points of weakness.

The church has another role in helping revise the crisis chapters of life. When we emerge, we are, it is hoped, "weller than well." God's grace has used the crisis for growth. The experience of victory is available to be shared with others who are in crisis.

And finally, the church has an ultimate contribution. Each book has an end, a closing chapter. Here the church is present to write not "Finished" but "To Be Continued in a New Dimension." The church militant in times of crises now announces that one of its own, through Christ, has joined the church triumphant!

9 Cancer Is Not Spelled D-E-A-T-H

The reaction of many people to the news that a relative or friend has cancer is such that you would think cancer is spelled D-E-A-T-H. "How much longer has he to live?" "Doctor, don't tell him he has cancer." To this atmosphere of doom the patient is likely to add his or her own questions. "Doctor, I'm not getting better, am I?" Statements such as these followed by evasive replies are our American equivalent of voodoo death dynamics.

Dr. W. L. Warner in a study of an Australian tribe shows how close friends and family can affect life adversely. In the case of the violation of a taboo, death is enhanced by the person's family:

> All normal social activity with him therefore ceases and he is left alone. Then, shortly before he dies, the group returns to him under the guidance of a ceremonial leader to perform mourning rites, the purpose of which is "to cut him off entirely from the ordinary world and ultimately place him . . . in . . . the . . . world . . . of the dead. . . . If all a man's near kin . . . business associates, friends, and all other members of the society, should suddenly withdraw themselves because of some dramatic circumstances . . . looking at the man as one already dead, and then after some little time perform over him a sacred ceremony believed with certainty to guide him out of the land of the living . . . the enormous suggestive power of this twofold movement of the community . . . can be somewhat understood by ourselves."[1]

[1] Quoted in Jerome Frank, *Persuasion and Healing* (New York: Schocken Books, Inc., 1963), pp. 40-41.

We can see in this tribe's behavior a parallel to our isolation of the cancer patient and our sending in a string of ministers to "save the soul." Withholding information from a strong person who has learned to handle crises can also produce a negative effect on the course of an illness, while truth can be a powerful healing tool. But often the patient sees the family members' discomfort and tries to protect them from the pain of anticipatory grief. The family members do the same for the patient, while secretly they all desire the openness they have always known in their relationship.

Who should visit the cancer patient? Those family and friends who can help the patient maintain hope, whose own lives are meaningful, and whose feelings are positive toward the ill person. The person with cancer should be encouraged to talk about himself or herself, especially about disappointments, failures, and recent drastic life-style changes, such as firing or retirement. If the person has lost a close loved one, grief counseling should assist in the reestablishing of warm relationships with others. And also the person should be able to talk about strengths, memories, goals, and the resources of faith.

Guilt should not be swept under the rug but acknowledged, and the person should be helped to know the experience of forgiveness by God and others. He or she needs a relationship of love, not condemnation for what has been done or for what he or she is like when at the weakest.

These suggestions may be very hard to follow. Strong emotions are involved in both patient and family. If you find you can't establish this open relationship on your own, talk with an understanding pastor or chaplain. Perhaps he or she can be your go-between.

Let us not abandon the person with cancer or offer a morbid relationship in which cancer is spelled D-E-A-T-H. Instead, let us offer a relationship that spells L-I-F-E. Even if the person dies physically, such a relationship helps in "tidying up" life's loose ends and making death easier. Furthermore, it helps the person grow closer to his or her potential. All this is possible because someone loves, and their love casts out the fear of death. A person with cancer can then pray: "We give thanks to God always for you all, constantly mentioning you in our prayers, remembering before our God and Father your work of faith and labor of love and steadfastness of hope in our Lord Jesus Christ" (1 Thessalonians 1:2-3).

10 Faith in . . .

Faith involves the head, the heart, the hands, and one's hope as life is lived in time. The elements of faith, like waves in the ocean, merge, grow, flow together, separate, and surface as each expresses its unique identity for a moment and again mingles with the sea, helping another wave to break upon the shoreline.

Belief is faith expressed through the mind. It is the energy of truth revealed by Christ who is the way, the truth, and the life (John 14:6). Jesus bears witness to the truth (John 5:33); we shall know the truth, and it will set us free (John 8:32). But how shall we know the truth that frees? The risen Christ, the Holy Spirit of Jesus will guide us into that freeing knowledge (John 16:13). Anyone committed to receiving the truth hears Jesus' voice (John 18:37). Would you turn a deaf ear to the truth that the God of this universe loves you, knows you, and will save you?

But faith is more than dry intellectualism. Faith is also a matter of the heart, of trust and love. Love and trust are emotional energies which are good for our body and spirit (soul). Trust is a warm heart. Trust is the assurance that, though all is not right without, God is within; and with him difficult matters *will* come out right.

Faith as a matter of the heart and love owes everything to God the lover. We love because God is the source of that love (John 15:9). We are to love one another as God has loved Jesus and as Jesus loves us.

By this kind of love people will know that we are Christians. The greatest love of all is that which gives its life for another person (see John 15:13).

Hope is not usually associated with an organ of the body (as love and the heart), but in the person's time dimension. It is inner power that permits us to tolerate pain in the present, to appreciate the present level of spiritual resources, and to press on to a better tomorrow. Even if tomorrow brings physical death, hope does not cease; like faith and love, it is eternal (1 Corinthians 13). Hope and belief are related. Hope is based on belief (John 5:45-47) and on experiences of love (Romans 5:1-5) that pass through the sequence of suffering, endurance, character, and hope. Hope and trust intermingle ". . . because God's love has been poured into our hearts through the Holy Spirit . . ." (Romans 5:5).

Faith expressed through the physical body is material energy supplied by God's providence as Father and Creator. He who gives us life and the truth by which we live also gives us the energy and direction (the way) to live. The "way" to live is a life of loving service. "He who has my commandments and keeps them, he it is who loves me; and he who loves me will be loved by my Father, and I will love him and manifest myself to him" (John 14:21). Belief, love, trust, and hope must find physical expression. God asks us to act before we have all the evidence. As we act upon the truth we know, God himself adds to belief, love, trust, and hope.

Faith is a relationship with God. Examining the parts moves us toward seeing the whole. Looking at faith's components is like looking at the different facets of a diamond ring. One brilliant flash may catch the eye. But one facet tells only a part; it must share its beauty with another facet, and so on around the diamond. But the diamond must be seen on the finger of a woman, and the finger that wears the ring must give way to the loving face and warm heart of she who wears it. And that love must share the stage with the loving heart of the man who gives the ring. The love of two for each other must in its turn point to the love of God. The flashing lights, the loving looks of lovers, the shared secrets—all acting together make more than the sum of the parts.

What is faith? Faith is a relationship so rich, so complex, so rewarding that words cannot describe it. Words can only invite another to try it. Won't you, today?

11 What Do We Expect to Happen?

". . . whatever you ask in prayer, believe that you have received it, and it will be yours" (Mark 11:24).

You can't teach an old dog new tricks.

It takes longer for old people to get well.

What do we expect to happen? How much mental programming goes on, and what is the effect upon the body of that mental image? It is an established scientific fact that a person under hypnosis can imagine that a harmless object is hot and raise a blister where the object touches the skin.

What do we expect to happen? How many times do we believe that something cannot be done, and we fulfill that belief by not trying? There is such a concept as a "self-fulfilling prophecy." Autosuggestion is a part of our human nature. We make suggestions to ourselves all day.

We know very well that the body is a fantastic chemical factory operating by chemical laws long recognized by physicians. Knowing this, much medical care is based upon the manipulation of body chemistry by external agents, such as drugs, heat, and physical therapy. We know so well that drugs work that we, without thought of the faith involved, fill a prescription or search the pharmacy shelves for the most powerful painkiller or the most effective heat rub for those sore muscles or arthritis. We *believe;* and the headache goes away, or the pulled muscle feels better. How much healing is in the aspirin, and how much healing is in the belief?

Perhaps an altered view of the body should accompany the older, accepted chemical view. The body is also an energy field. There appear to be several forms of energy essential for human life: light for creation and re-creation; love for growth, moral energy, or truth; and power or physical energy.

Perhaps there are other energy forms, but for now let us look at light. The Hebrew word used for the light on the first day of creation is different from the Hebrew word for the light coming from the sun and moon on the fourth day of creation. This first day creation light has been associated with healing energy. Agnes Sanford in her book *The Healing Light* equates healing power and light. Others who have a ministry of healing through prayer on occasion use the imagery of light. In Disneyland my wife and I took an interesting ride in which we were progressively "shrunk" in size. In succession we were surrounded by beautiful crystals, molecules, atoms, the nucleus of an atom, and finally by gentle pulsations of light. This had a quieting effect; we felt at peace, indeed, at one with the very essence of creation with God who manifests himself as light. His Son said, "I am the light of the world."

Perhaps in addition to seeing our bodies as subject only to the slower chemical changes, we should see also our kinship with the God of healing light, whose power can affect us at a more basic level—that of the spirit.

"Faith healing is the healing of one's faith," says Edgar Jackson. And there are many people who believe that this healing is prior to physical healing. We who believe so readily that an aspirin can cure our headache should work at the belief that God's energy at work in our spirit is prior to any physical healing efforts. "What do you expect to happen?" is a question to be considered along with "Do you want to get well?"

12 The Wisdom Beyond That of Education

His mastery of English would not allow him to pass a third grade English test. But he could communicate his thoughts and feelings perfectly. He obviously had little formal education, but he was wise, very wise to the art of living. He was a sixty-two-year-old man from a nearby rural community who was recovering from a heart attack.

I listened to his sad story. A private businessman, he had had a heart attack five years before. He had no insurance and was too ill to resume work. Having too much pride to accept welfare as well as too many financial resources to qualify, he told a story of declining health and the slow drain of his resources. Now this second heart attack found him owning only a small farmhouse on a couple of acres of land.

He made a strong impression on on me primarily because of his victorious attitude. He also impressed me with his understanding of the task of crisis resolution. I can still hear his words in the dialect of that area. "You has to make peace with what you has lost, and you has to do the best you kin with what you has left."

Two lessons can be drawn from this man's life. First, his comment on handling crises is profound. In a crisis we frequently lose something important, such as our strong heart, our vocation, or our marriage. This loss can frequently set into motion a series of losses. In his case the heart attack led to the loss of his business, which in turn led to the loss of financial independence; and undoubtedly the stress associated with these losses contributed to the second heart attack. In a crisis we also have deep feelings associated with loss. Grief feelings include anger, guilt, anxiety, and sadness. We can feel very insecure, helpless, and hopeless. Therefore, part of the crisis is in looking back, making peace, that is, dealing with the grief associated with loss. ("Working" with the emotions associated with memories is an important task in mourning, but, of course, it is not to continue as a substitute for responsible decision making and living in the present day.)

A crisis also has a forward look, with two groups of emotions. One is associated with the anxiety of not knowing where to turn or what to do. But there are also strong supportive emotions associated with hope for a better tomorrow and the support of family and friends. We need not only learn to do the best we can with what we have left, but we also need to look for new resources and goals. Life, if it is to go on, must be meaningful, and we must invest life's energies in new purposes and activities which are possible within newly imposed restricted physical and emotional conditions. We may no longer move mountains with our bulldozer, but could that experience in moving mountains be used to teach young people in trade school to move mountains? The question is suggestive of the kind of "spiritual homework" made possible by the spirit of hope. Usually concentration upon the possibilities of new opportunities to use one's life is more helpful to a suffering person than the catharsis of expressing one's anxieties and problems. Analyzing and searching for solutions is also an answer to the frequent experience of getting bogged down in negative feelings and thoughts. Find reasons and resources for living, and they will chase away anxiety, doubt, hopelessness, and fear. Darkness cannot withstand light.

The second lesson is the fulfillment of prophecy in this man. In Acts 2:17-18, Joel 2:28 is fulfilled. In Joel we are told that everybody, especially young men and women, shall prophesy. Those who are uneducated, as well as priest and prophet, shall be filled with God's Spirit. Profound Holy Spirit wisdom was prominent in this elderly man who lacked the wisdom of formal education. And, I, a Christian clergyman engaged in professional crisis counseling, suddenly found myself blessed (see Matthew 11:25) by a simple and Spirit-filled man.

The point to which these thoughts move is that in a crisis we should not live in the past via memory and wishes for the restoration of the "good ol' days." Nor are we to be suspended in the present by magical wishes and deliverance dreams of a more perfect tomorrow. None of this past and future time consciousness will do. A crisis is an active time of spiritual communion with God who helps us make peace with what we have lost (mourning) and who actively explores with us in prayer and in our normal thought processes the resources and reasons for living. That is, he helps us do the best we can with what we have left and helps us recognize and appropriate new resources and ministries of loving service.

And that is a *promise* (prophecy) made by God himself. Claim it!

13 Unbalanced Society and Unbalanced People

David was a handsome man, prominent in his profession. But David was forty-five years old and bothered by life changes. His "mid-life transition" was manageable until tragedy struck. When he tried to put his life back together again, he discovered he did not have all the pieces. That's when he turned to his "preacher."

David invites you to reflect upon his experience. There may be something you can learn from his pain, something that may save you from a similar, painful lesson. Honestly answer for yourself some questions David put to himself.

1. Is the life you experience through the senses real? How do you develop this part of yourself? Spa workouts? Jogging? Do you read books that help you become a connoisseur of good foods and wines? This life experienced through the senses—what are its joys and pains?

2. If you said "yes" to the first part of item 1, you will probably also be inclined to say, "Yes, the *social order* is real." How do you develop your social skills? Do you read the latest "girlie" magazines or woman's magazines in order to learn how to: (1) "make it" in the business world; (2) "make out" (illicitly) with another person's spouse; (3) "bug out" of present commitments in order to advance over someone else? This life experienced through the social order—what are its joys and pains, and how do you deal with its brokenness?

It is easy to say, "Yes, the life we experience through the senses and the social order is real." Philosophy and the physical and behavioral sciences have examined this part of reality in great detail. Furthermore, it is highly visible, seems substantial, and yields to our control. But is this *all* there is to life? Are we merely magnificent, sensuous, social animals? Some would say "yes" and seek no more until tragedy strikes, such as the death of a spouse or child, or until the person is the victim of unjust, undeserved evil inflicted by another person.

3. The next step in David's "life review" involved a series of related questions. Are values important to life? Is there meaning in life? Do we have a destiny beyond this life in the flesh?

If you answered "yes" to one or more of these questions in item 3, you are no longer merely a humanist. You are now a *theist* and a *humanist*. It is only a short step from these questions to acknowledging that the two great commandments given by Jesus are at the very heart of reality. He said we are to love God first and then our neighbor:

> And one of the scribes came up and heard them disputing with one another, and seeing that he answered them well, asked him, "Which commandment is the first of all?" Jesus answered, "The first is, 'Hear, O Israel: The Lord our God, the Lord is one; and you shall love the Lord your God with all your heart, and with all your soul, and with all your mind, and with all your strength.' The second is this, 'You shall love your neighbor as yourself.' There is no other commandment greater than these" (Mark 12:28-31).

As David discussed with his pastor the spiritual dimensions of his life, he emphasized how difficult his social and business acquaintances made it for him to be religious. He observed that our society was unbalanced and helped to create unbalanced citizens. David's pastor responded by telling how spiritual experiences have "gone public" and can no longer be ignored. They are being studied by the very sciences which so long neglected them. Parapsychology, for example, is now recognized as a legitimate science. Today people talk openly about "out-of-body" experiences; before they did so only by risking being called "crazy." A leading researcher in death and dying testifies that she now believes in immortality.

Meditation groups designed only for personal and social growth sometimes go beyond their intention and reveal experiences of the holy. Awe and reverence, holy love and joy become a part of the lives of those formerly content to be merely sensuous and social animals. These experiences have led to great research efforts. Meditation has come out of the Christian monastery and returned as a spiritual discipline for the devout lay person.

Faith healing is now assuming greater importance as the church pays closer attention to Jesus' healing ministry and realizes that the gift can be used by devout Christians.

Sigmund Freud, who treated religious visions as illusions and pathology, is losing credibility to one of his students, Carl Jung, the greatest psychological researcher of the religious life. Indeed, transpersonal psychology is a prominent "growing edge" in today's psychological research.

What can we say to all like David who are unbalanced? First, *evaluate your life*. What are your priorities? Carry a notebook and keep a daily log for one month. How much time is given to business, family and social relationships, recreation and religious activities? What are you leaving out?

Second, *correct the unbalance*. Join a church school class or church for spiritual growth; go camping (if your life is too full of people); play your neglected favorite sport or develop a new one. Your profession may need to wait while your marriage catches up or you get to know your children. In other words, a short-term overshift in priorities may be in order, followed by a long-term shift to a more balanced life.

Third, *find a group of people who will reinforce your efforts to be a balanced person*. You might start with a nearby church if you don't have one. After all, the root meaning of religion—*religio*—is "to bind together." When one's life has been shattered or unbalanced, faith has the power to restore a sense of unity. One warning though—some Christian groups are themselves unbalanced. They may espouse body-denying and pie-in-the-sky theologies, or they could be cults or sects promising love and community at the exhorbitant price of surrendering personal freedom and responsibility.

Make the keystone of your efforts belief in a God of love who wishes to "be for you" and to express his love through your love. God wants all people to love one another as he has loved us.

HEALTHY LIVING AND ILLNESS PREVENTION

14 Jesus, Hygeia, and Aesculapius

Jesus healed a man ill for thirty-eight years. He said to the man, "See, you are well! Sin no more, that nothing worse befall you" (John 5:14). Two very important principles for a holistic approach to health and healing are found here. First, there is the healing itself. Second, a prescription is given for maintaining healthful living. Another healing with a positive prescription is given in Jesus' healing of the demoniac to whom he commanded a witnessing life-style (Mark 5:1-20).

This twofold approach to health and healing was also recognized by the ancient Greeks. In their "many-gods" approach (polytheism) to religion they separated the two principles. Hygeia was the goddess of health or the life force. Hygeia could also be called the *goddess of illness prevention*. The Greek *god of healing,* Aesculapius, is better known than his daughter Hygeia. He had temples where one could go for healing. Dreams one had while sleeping in the temple, healing snakes, surgery, and herbal medicine were prominent healing modalities. A contemporary symbol of the medical profession, the caduceus, showing two snakes weaving around a rod, is a reminder in the form of an ancient symbol of the natural union of religion and medicine.

In the last half of the twentieth century the healing arts of Aesculapius are quite advanced. The church has lent its resources to the medical establishment primarily in the form of hospital sponsorship and in the provision of chaplaincy services. Like the lesser-known goddess Hygeia, the Christian principle of prevention of illness and maintenance of health by the incarnation of the Spirit of God goes largely unnoticed.

The role of the church in health maintenance and prevention of illness goes on in its educational, worship, and support ministries. But the benefits from these activities cannot be measured and so, often go unnoticed. Also, their purpose in promoting physical and mental health is often not realized. When we lose sight of *why* we do what we do, we quit doing it. Then, in the absence of the blessing, we realize what we have lost and restore the activity necessary to obtain the blessing.

A problem often seen in stress-related illnesses is the person's return again and again to the physician and hospitals. Many times the treatment is the best traditional medicine can give, and that, often, is only symptomatic relief. Hygeia needs a larger role in the temples of Aesculapius. Jesus' message, "Sin no more," in our modern terminology is an invitation to change one's life-style as a means of reducing illness and, in turn, medical costs.

While the church's work with the principle of Aesculapius is important, its major contribution to health and healing in the immediate future may be in issuing a prophetic call to all people and institutions to give greater opportunity to the principle of Hygeia.

> And as he was getting into the boat, the man who had been possessed with demons begged him that he might be with him. But he refused, and said to him, "Go home to your friends, and tell them how much the Lord has done for you, and how he has had mercy on you." And he went away and began to proclaim in the Decapolis how much Jesus had done for him; and all men marveled (Mark 5:18-20).

15 The Illness-Prevention God

> *"If you will diligently hearken to the voice of the LORD your God, and do that which is right in his eyes, and give heed to his commandments and keep all his statutes, I will put none of the diseases upon you which I put upon the Egyptians; for I am the LORD, your healer"* (Exodus 15:26).

What do quarantine, sun, running water, fire, fresh air, worship and the fear of God have in common? Infection control. Moses belongs in the company of Pasteur and Lister, medical researchers in infection control. Indeed, many of today's sanitary and illness-prevention measures can be shown to be similar to the same principles upon which Mosaic laws are based.

What were they? Moses' law included washing the body and clothes in *running water* (a shower is cleaner than a bath). He instructed that the upper lip be covered (a face mask to prevent the spread of airborne germs?) and that certain sick persons be banished from the community (isolation?). The law required the burning or washing of contaminated clothing (secondary infection controls?). An unclean condition lasted until sundown (to give the sun's ultraviolet rays adequate time to complete their work of sterilization?). And finally, persons were inspected by a priest (health officer for the community?).

Add to the previous measures the laws (health regulations) applied to persons who handled dead bodies. These included the washing or breaking of uncovered cooking pots which were near the body and the washing of the body during seven days of uncleanliness (isolation?) (Numbers 19:11-22). Also certain unclean ''swarming creatures'' are listed, among them, the mouse. If a mouse got in a pot of food, the food was thrown away and the pot was washed or broken (Leviticus

11:29-38). The sanitary disposal of human excrement is found in Deuteronomy 23:12-13. The remedy is so simple—bury it. The commandment to keep the sabbath from work shows the recreation of a rhythm of work and rest.

Many of the biblical reasons given for these health matters are ceremonial. The ancient Hebrew probably knew nothing of cholesterol and germs. The interesting thing is that the instructions still stand, though today we have discovered through scientific research different reasons to honor them. Old Testament dietary and sanitary laws served (and still serve) the need for prevention of illness. In those ancient times, when you became ill, you faced the prospect of limited means of cure; so it was essential that you not get sick. This is true even today. It is better not to have a stroke or heart attack or diabetes. Today healing is an advanced art; but today the cost has become so great that few can afford to get sick! Prevention is part of the religious heritage that is assuming increased importance today, for the old and for a new reason.[1]

An occasional theologian may reason that God is dead, and many secularists may live as though he is dead; but he continues to reveal his love to those who *live* and *reason* their faith. His love comes in unexpected ways. Today we are rediscovering an ancient way—prevention. God calls modern-day prophets and researchers as well as "ordinary" citizens to a study of the Bible. This blend of spiritual wisdom and modern research will surely bless us richly.

God wants us to have abundant life. That life includes health and freedom from unnecessary suffering. Both prevention and healing are blessings from the "Lord, your healer" (Exodus 15:26).

---

[1] This material is adapted from Rudolph E. Grantham, *Lay Shepherding* (Valley Forge, Pa.: Judson Press, 1980), pp. 89-90.

16 The Message from the Rabbit Town Church Cemetery

The Rabbit Town church cemetery had received the dead of its rural north Alabama community for over 145 years at the time I was committing Granny's body to the earth that had sustained her for ninety-six years. The newer graves were on the far back side, and no roads were cut to them. As we walked behind Granny Borden's casket, I was appalled at the large number of short graves; many measured only two or three feet between the crude headstones and footstones. Most of the fieldstone markers had no names cut into them. The identities of their occupants are known only to God.

After the funeral I shared my observation with my father-in-law. He responded by saying that life was hard on children when the area was first settled. Life was also hard on the adults; my mother-in-law pulled an old, yellowed newspaper article from the strongbox. The *Anniston Star* had printed an article on Granny's father-in-law, the oldest man in Calhoun County: he was sixty years old!

These two vignettes show how health care has changed. Thanks to immunizations and laws requiring them for preschool children, and thanks to research in drugs and advanced surgical and life-support techniques, many people are adults before they bury a close family member. No longer do many die from childhood diseases or from pneumonia and other infectious diseases. Many dreaded illnesses of yesteryear are routinely treated in the doctor's office.

What we see today is an increase of a new class of diseases. The conclusion of impressive research evidence is that this new class of illnesses is associated with stress. And behind the stress we see a connection to changes in values and life-styles; these changes inflict these illnesses. Some day it may also be proved to the medical researchers' satisfaction that stress illness is associated with the breakdown in supportive relationships normally found in the family and community. If you listen to people talk about their illnesses, you may find that they readily make the association. Thus we inflict these illnesses upon ourselves and have lost a preventative measure for these illnesses.

Medical research based upon nineteenth-century methodology, values, and assumptions about the nature of creation has made great contributions. But medicine is in a transition stage. Many of our health problems have been solved; let us rejoice! But the old ways do not work well on stress illnesses. Instead, American medicine is rediscovering old values and researching new methods, such as relaxation and the medical use of hypnosis, meditation, and visualization.

Medicine in the last quarter of the twentieth century is rapidly turning from fragmentation to holism and synthesis. What is included in this holistic concept varies from person to person. For example, the federal government sees the person only as a sick social animal and fails to consider a divine element in human nature. But one element is being emphasized in both secular and spiritual holism: *personal responsibility for maintaining one's own health and for regaining it when ill.*

No prior civilization has exposed itself to such a variety of toxic chemicals. We can destroy our lungs with nicotine, our brains with LSD, and our livers with alcohol. And these are just a few self-induced illnesses. We can change our mood with "uppers" and come down with "downers." It is our choice in these cases.

But sometimes the choice is someone else's, and innocent people suffer. "No one is going to tell me I cannot smoke pot!" "After a couple of joints and beers," read the police accident report, "the man rammed another car, killing a young couple and a child." Manslaughter charges were filed and after a long legal battle, a judge refused justice to the dead and released the young man because his rights had been violated by a "lack of due process." Individualism and freedom of expression are important values, but not when isolated from the value of responsibility to one's neighbor. This story not only illustrates that we are responsible for our health and consciousness but also that we are responsible for the potential consequences of our behavior on others (the judge in this case notwithstanding).

We are also responsible for our own health care when ill. It is so elementary as to seem foolish to say this; but some people refuse to see a doctor when they are ill, and some refuse the best medical advice. Many end up beautiful young corpses. Our doctor can do little when our will is to be ill. The medical establishment can work with the body's own natural healing powers and with the Great Physician *only* when we invite its intervention.

The children in the nineteenth-century Rabbit Town community had little choice when they became ill. Medicine in their day could not cure many of their illnesses. How different things are today, when we deliberately starve our body and feed it poisons in the name of culture, customs, and an "everybody is doing it" value. We choose death; they could not choose life.

Did the demoniac and the man healed at the Beth-zatha pool live a different life-style, as Jesus' commanded? We don't know. The Bible is silent on this question. But the Bible does tell us that Jesus recognized the relationship between life-style and its values, on the one hand and illness and prevention on the other. In this regard he anticipated holistic medicine by almost 2,000 years when he stated his mission's priorities in Luke 4:16-21:

> And he came to Nazareth, where he had been brought up; and he went to the synagogue, as his custom was, on the sabbath day. And he stood up to read; and there was given to him the book of the prophet Isaiah. He opened the book and found the place where it was written,
>
> > "The Spirit of the Lord is upon me,
> > because he has anointed me to
> > preach good news to the poor.
> > He has sent me to proclaim release
> > to the captives
> > and recovering of sight to the blind,
> > to set at liberty those who are oppressed,
> > to proclaim the acceptable year of the Lord."

And he closed the book, and gave it back to the attendant, and sat down; and the eyes of all in the synagogue were fixed on him. And he began to say to them, "Today this scripture has been fulfilled in your hearing" (Luke 4:16-21).

17 The Good Earth

*"I will restore health to you,
and your wounds I will heal. . . ."*
—Jeremiah 30:17

It was a good weekend! We arrived at the "Shack" on Friday afternoon with enough daylight left to pick beans, cut okra and squash, and pick blueberries. That night, sitting on the porch, we enjoyed the farm pond chorus and the woodland symphony. The full moon cast deep shadows, giving the imagination room to play.

Next morning the sunlight nudged us awake, and after a leisurely breakfast we went blackberry picking. The picking was interrupted by the neighboring farmer telling us that pine pulpwood harvesters were working on the next farm and had run out the rattlesnakes. Furthermore, he had killed two himself—be careful in those berry bushes! My back, by then, felt as if it would break; so I welcomed the opportunity to check the Georgia longleaf pine seedlings laboriously planted the year before. Growth was visible as was my joy in being a successful tree farmer.

My daughter had a zillion questions on as many discoveries, and my wife and I, while shelling peas, caught up on current family problems and redreamed hopes and plans for the future.

Lunch couldn't be beat. It felt good to eat a plate of fried chicken surrounded by my own homegrown vegetables. Finally, after a nap, we had an uneventful trip home and went to bed with a pleasantly tired feeling.

All these relaxing, getting-away type experiences lead us to a spiritual truth. There is a rhythm in life: work—rest; activity—passivity, giving—receiving. That which has been well used must be rested. That which is not used we lose. Such a rhythm is restoring and relaxing and healing.

Another restoring experience of that weekend was "getting back to nature," or getting close to the soil from which we are made. This experience of renewal through nature and the Creator God is the subject of the myth involving a fight between Hercules and Antaeus, the son of Gaea, Mother Earth. You may recall that Antaeus had the ability to regain his strength by touching earth with his feet. Every time Hercules knocked him down, Antaeus leaped up renewed. Finally, Hercules realized the secret and won the fight by holding Antaeus high in the air.

Myths are entertaining ways of teaching a subtle truth, but the sacred history of Scripture is more convincing for many Christians. Here we can see God renewing those who wait upon him. Poetically, Isaiah describes them: "They will rise on wings like eagles . . ." (40:31, TEV). Elijah's encounter with God followed a dramatic confrontation with Jezebel. God in a still, small voice gave comfort and instruction for further mission (1 Kings 19:9-18).

For the Christian, the detailed Gospels show Jesus' life-style of work alternating with frequent retreats into the wilderness for prayer and renewal. In the solitude of nature Jesus conversed with God. On one occasion, the experience was so real, we are told, that his face was radiant and his clothing became dazzling white (see Luke 9:29).

If we are to know strength adequate to the stresses of modern living, it may be that, like Antaeus, we must place our feet on the earth: hike a nature trail or go fishing or go camping. In physical exertion, in leisurely conversation with spouse, children, or friends, and in prayer we will find our whole being strengthened. And God's word to Jeremiah will be God's word to us as well:

> "I will restore health to you
> and your wounds I will heal."

And we might also add that such a life-style will *keep* us healthy.

COMPLETING ONE'S HEALING

18 Life Review

> . . . *the mind of a wise man will know the time and way. For every matter has its time and way, although man's trouble lies heavy upon him* (Ecclesiastes 8:5-6).

I first visited the woman in the coronary care unit. Not knowing her religious affiliation, I asked if she had a pastor whom I could call. "No," she said, "I was raised a Methodist, became a Baptist, married a Jew and tried out Jewish [*sic*], and I'm now a bad Catholic."

"In that case," I replied, "I offer you my pastoral services. The hospital provides a chaplain for patients who do not have a minister."

"Oh, if *you* want to visit me, that's fine," she responded. I did, for I saw in her three marriages and multiple attempts at finding a faith a deep need to be committed to something or somebody worthy, perhaps even committed to herself.

On another day she was in a regular nursing unit and was standing looking out the window. The light outlined her features in stark black and white. I could tell she was in a reflective mood. "A penny for your thoughts," I said.

She turned to me and replied, "They aren't worth that much." She sat down and motioned for me to take the other chair.

I began the conversation with, "It has been my experience that people with your illness often engage in a life review. Is that what's going on now with you?"

"Yes, I've had a lot of time to think. Reverend, my religious life is all screwed up. I've screwed up my life, too, and I can't undo a thing!" She cried softly, and I waited.

Illness removes us from the rush of modern life. It gives us time to think. And we do—we reflect and plan, pray and repent, cry and try to repair what is broken. The wise person also releases the past to God's mercy and accepts the consequences of prior decisions. With the experience gained from the lessons of the past, the wise person will look for resources and God's guidance for the future.

Time taken for a life review is like the laying of the foundation for a new building. That building should be our private temple for God's spirit. Two things are necessary if we are to do our spiritual homework well. A life review demands that we *have* a good listener and that we *be* a good listener.

"A friend," says one definition, "is one who knows all about you and is still your friend." A friend is one who knows how and when to support you when you're down or deflate your ego when you are too high. A friend will not "yes" your illusions but will help you see reality. A life review is more effective with a good friend or pastor who takes time to listen.

A successful life review also demands that we *be* a good listener. We must honestly listen to the response of our friend and evaluate his or her wisdom; a friend is fallible. But we must also listen to God. Meditative prayer is basically *listening*. Often God whispers and can be heard only in a "closet" (see Matthew 6:6) or a "cave" (1 Kings 19:9-14).

In meditative prayer we relax and fill our consciousness with the presence of God or Christ. Also helpful are images of biblical scenes and symbols of spiritual reality (the rainbow, shepherds, clouds, etc.). In this sense of oneness we place our problem before God. Quietly and patiently we listen. We may also dialogue about the images we receive and thank him for answering our prayer.

Then we act out the answer. It is not enough to give it over to God and say, "*You* take care of it." "Let God do it" and "Let George do it" are both forms of irresponsibility. We must take the necessary action to alter the life-limiting situation. That is the last step in our life review. And it is hoped that, like Elijah, we will return to life renewed and with a new mission.

For many people, sickness forces a life review in which we listen and someone listens to us. This dialogue of love and shared wisdom in the company of the Great Physician is the means by which we pass through our troubles to victory.

19 When Tragedy Takes Away a Strength

Jesus, in a loud voice, commanded, "Lazarus, come out!" (John 11:43). Did Jesus address a body of flesh, dead for four days, as Martha thought? What did Jesus address when he called Lazarus's name? *What* associated with the name "Lazarus" responded?

I think these questions are related to our concept of human nature. Very often we identify ourselves with only a part of ourselves: with a strong gift or talent (star football player, beauty queen) or with a pleasant role (lover, nurturing mother). We spend much time, money, and thought developing and using that talent or role.

We have a body; we are not a body. We have feelings, but we are not our feelings. We have a mind, but we are not our intellect. We have a vocation but we are not judge, preacher, or teacher. We have husband or wife, father or mother roles, but we are not Mom or Pop. We are more than one part or role and more than the sum of our parts and roles.

How we see ourselves when a crisis strikes, determines, in part, how we cope. The last child leaves home, and a mother skids into a depression. She never considers the option of going to college and pursuing a postponed career. "Mr. Company President" is fired at fifty-five and destroys his life through alcohol. "Preacher" takes all criticism of the institutional church as a personal attack and collapses under what he interprets as personal rejection.

Death is the ultimate crisis which tests our self-concept. These thoughts are part of my personal grief work. Just one week prior to this writing, my father-in-law was buried. At the funeral home I did not ask to see Mr. B. I asked where Mr. B.'s body lay in state. "Pop" is alive. And I believe Jesus in the Lazarus resurrection is saying that this "I" is immortal. The life energies of the spiritual self, or the "I," seem to be intimately connected with breath—the breath of God, the Holy Spirit. The "I" inhabits flesh but survives the death of our physical body.

If we are not merely our parts, what are we? What is this consciousness that can stand back and look at our parts and the roles we play? This self-consciousness has been named "self," "spirit," "ego," "I." Perhaps this "I" is so intangible as to be beyond description. Or perhaps we do not have language adequate to the task.

Nevertheless, it seems safe to affirm that this "I" directs all the parts and roles we play. A basic principle of the theory and therapy of psychosynthesis is: *"We are dominated by everything with which our self becomes identified. We can dominate and control everything from which we dis-identify ourselves."*[1] This means that when a part of my self is in trouble, all other parts share in the trouble. But it also means that the "I" can call upon the strengths of the parts to find a new synthesis.

For example, Mr. Company President has been fired at fifty-five. Of course, he is in grief, perhaps shock, too, if he did not anticipate the firing. But he did not rise to this position through luck. The essential being of this man, his "I," can call upon his body of knowledge, his lifetime of discipline, his prior problem-solving techniques, his business contacts, and his character to rise above the crisis.

My loved one is dead. And though Jesus is not here to call his name and unite his "I" with his body, I can be sure that my loved one lives and that my own spiritual "I" can call forth all that I am to mourn his loss, to celebrate his life of love among us, and his triumphant life. This is my witness, for in this day I shall know the fulfillment of Isaiah's prophecy:

> Your sun shall no more go down,
> nor your moon withdraw itself;
> for the LORD will be your everlasting light,
> and your days of mourning shall be ended.
> —Isaiah 60:20

---

[1] Roberto Assagioli, *Psychosynthesis* (New York: The Viking Press, Penguin Books, 1976), p. 22.

20 When Death Completes a Healing

"I am the Alpha and the Omega," says the Lord God, who is and who was and who is to come, the Almighty (Revelation 1:8).

Death is always the ultimate winner in its conflict with healing. But salvation vanquishes the sting of death. Jesus Christ is healer and Savior. Even death serves his purposes, as we see in this story of victory over death.

The operator's voice had an urgent tone to it as she gave the cardiopulmonary resuscitation code and location for the CPR team. The chaplain always answers this code and offers support to the family.

A woman unexpectedly developed heart trouble. She had been recovering from minor surgery and was to go home the next day. When I arrived, the family told me the following story.

The doctor had just left the room. The mother said, "Look, Son, Dad is here!" (The husband had been dead for several years, I later learned.) "Dad, Son made it home." (Her son lived out of town and had come to visit his mother in her illness.) "It is so *beautiful*." To the daughter-in-law, she asked, "Take Son to church." To her son, "Son, kiss me." He kissed his mother on the forehead. "No Son, like you did when a little boy, hug me." He kissed his mother and hugged her. "Dad is here and I have to go. It is so green and beautiful." She closed her eyes and gasped for breath.

The son called for the nurse and said that his mother was dead. The nurse and the patient's doctor ran into the room and began cardiopulmonary resuscitation. "Do what you can," said the son excitedly as he and his wife were ushered out of the room.

They discussed the CPR team's efforts with me and then agreed that all efforts to revive her should be stopped. Her death was so beautiful that they felt CPR was against God's will. At that moment the patient's bed was pushed down the hall to the coronary care unit. The daughter-in-law tried to run after it, yelling, "Don't do that; she asked not to go in there!" Her husband stopped her. A daughter then arrived, and her brother told her the account of the mother's death.

I went into the coronary care unit to check on progress. By this time the details of the woman's last vision had spread throughout the hospital staff. A doctor helping with the CPR came out of the room and said, "We ought not to be doing this" (the CPR). I left only to be met at the door by the woman's daughter. She said, "Please, I must talk to the nurse."

"They are all busy," I replied.

"Tell them not to hook her to any machines. The family does not want it, and she asked that it not be done." I returned to the unit and told this to the doctor.

"She is dead" he replied.

I carried the message to the daughter, and the family went with me to the chapel. After funeral arrangements had been made, I accompanied the son and his wife to the mother's room. They talked to her lifeless body and kissed it.

"Chaplain," said the daughter-in-law, "she asked only one thing: that I bring my husband to church."

"Chaplain," said the man, "it is beautiful up there." He pointed his finger and looked up. "Mother said it was beautiful!" He cried softly as he walked out. There was an unusual quietness and light about us. I went to my office and thanked God for blessing me by letting me be present with this family.

The grace of the Lord Jesus Christ and the love of God and the fellowship of the Holy Spirit be with you all (2 Corinthians 13:14).